LEARN TO READ PHONETICALLY COLLECTION 8

Compounds
with Silent e Words

Written by Mary Schuler

Illustrated by Nicholas Torres

Collection 8: This is a collection of four stories that builds on the previous collections by adding <u>Compound</u> words. The first two stories are written with the *Dolch phonetic Sight Words and those words that can be combined to form a compound word. The next two stories add other compound words. Each story will have a list of vocabulary words at the beginning as well as questions to answer at the end.

*The 315 Dolch Sight Vocabulary list is taken from the Picture Word Cards and Popper Words Set 1 (included in item #0-07-609422-7), plus Popper Words Set 2 (#0-07-602539-X) published by SRA (1-888-SRA-4543 or SRAonline.com).

NEXT BOOK

Collection 9: This is a collection of five stories, building from the previous collections by adding the <u>DOLCH Vowel Reference Card</u> words. Each story will have a list of vocabulary words at the beginning as well as questions to answer at the end.

DEDICATION

These books were created for children to help them learn how to read by using phonics skills systematically. These books are dedicated to parents, giving them an early literacy practical guide with tools.

ACKNOWLEDGMENTS

These books were created for _Schuler Phonics CORE (Second Part)_, authored by Mary M. Schuler. This collection includes Companion Stories #34-37.

It is highly recommended that BEFORE reading this book, your child/student should study the following sections in <u>Schuler Phonics CORE (Second Part)</u> Vowel Reference Card by Mary M. Schuler:

1. Single Consonants with Short Vowels
2. The FLOSS and CK Rule
3. Adding s and 's to nouns and verbs
4. Blends with Short Vowels
5. Digraphs with Short Vowels
6. Adding es to nouns ending s, x, z, ch, or sh
7. The Silent e Rule and
8. Compound Words

<u>www.parentreadingcoach.org</u>
FOR TRAINING VIDEOS

Schuler Phonics and Companion Books WHERE "Sound it out" really works!

But to help it work, note the following:

Any word _italicized_/_underlined_ in these stories should NOT be sounded out --- because sounding out just won't work on those words! (A, a, The, the will not be italicized/underlined even though considered "non-phonetic"; there are just too many of them, and they really are not a problem!)

Note: "Sound it out" doesn't always work --- because there are lots of words that can't be sounded out unless a person knows "millions and millions" of phonetic rules.

Why Schuler Phonics works: Schuler Phonics only teaches the basic, most common rules and then uses words based on those rules, all of which then can be sounded out.

For the stories in this collection your child should learn the following underlined/italicized words and parts of words by sight (Do NOT sound out --- It doesn't work!):

are	_house_	_some/where_
back/_door_	in/_put_	thank-_you_
come	in/_to_	the
_do_	_live_ (short i)	_their_
does	_lives_ (short i)	_there_
dog/_house_	_of_	_they_
doll/_house_	_once_	_to_
done	_one_	_two_
door	on/_to_	_u/pon_
door/bell	_out/put_	_walk_
door/stop	_put_	_want_
eight	_said_	_wants_
fire/_house_	_school_	_watch_
floor	_school/house_	_were_
goes	_some_	_where_
have	_some/one_	_who_
hen/_house_	_some_/thing	_you_
hot/_house_	_some_/time	_your_

Plus (phonics concepts not yet introduced).

a	_be_	_kind_
a/cross	_both_	_my_
a/like	_by_	_my_/self
a/live (long i)	_for_	_no_
all	_for_/get	_or_
a/long	_for_/got	_out_
a/rise	_from_	_was_
a/wake	_go_	_we_
a/while	_he_	_what_
a/woke	_I_	

All the other words can be sounded out as they are based on short vowel and single consonant, blend, and digraph words, silent e rule, plus compound words.

IMPORTANT NOTE FOR PARENTS/TEACHERS:

A or **a** should NOT be pronounced as long a (/ā/ as in the word say) in the phrase/sentence such as, "Once upon **a** time," or "Mom got **a** fish." Instead, **A** or **a** should be pronounced as a short u (/ŭ/ as in umbrella /ŭ/ or up /ŭ/).

The e in the words **The** or **the** should NOT be pronounced as long e (/ē/ as in the word bee) in the phrase such as "**The** Milkman's Cap," or "No, it is not **the** milkman." Instead the e in **The** or **the** should be pronounced as a short u (/ŭ/ as in umbrella /ŭ/ or up /ŭ/).

CONTENTS

Dolch Sight Words ONLY

Other Phonetic Words

STORY 1: DOLCH SIGHT WORDS

The Milkman's Cap

COMPANION STORY 34
DOLCH SIGHT WORDS

Non-phonetic Dolch sight words:

are	_one_	_u/pon_
come	_put_	_want_
_do_	_said_	_wants_
done	_some_	_were_
door	_some/one_	_where_
goes	the	_who_
have	_their_	_you_
in/_to_	_there_	_your_
_of_	_to_	
once	_two_	

Phonetic Dolch sight words (BUT phonics concepts not yet introduced):

a	_for_	_kind_
a/like	_for_/get	_my_
a/live (long i)	_for_/got	_no_
a/long	_from_	_was_
_by_	_I_	

Phonetic words (but not Dolch):

camp	mmmm	still
camp/fire	mom	stripe
dad	Mom	stripes
Dad	more	time
fat	pan	wet
glad	sad	
lake		

Dolch vocabulary to practice:

1. Before reading these words, write a list of the silent e words or have your mom or dad write the list while you read just the silent e words below. HINT: There will be an e at the end of the word, but watch out, there might be an s or an 's added to the word after the e. WARNING: Some silent e words are hidden in a compound word.

2. Then read the words from the list in the back of the book while your mom or dad checks if you put each word on your list. Did you find them all?

and	drink	its	sun/fish
at	fire	jump	sun/up
ate	fish	just	take
back	fishes	let	takes
best	gave	like	that
black	get	likes	them
black/fish	gets	live (long i)	these
blue	got	long	top
blue/fish	had	long-jump	up
but	hand	man	us
came	has	man's	went
can	here	milk	when
can/not	his	milk/man	white
cap	hot	milk/man's	white/fish
cat	hot/dog	not	with
Cat	hot/dogs	on	with/in
cat/fish	in	red	yes
did	in/let	red/fish	
dog	is	stick	
dogs	it	sun	

The sun is up. _Once_ _upon_ a time, at sunup, _there_ _was_ _someone_ with a milkman's cap on top _who_ got a pan _of_ milk _for_ the cat. Is it the milkman? _No_, it is not the milkman. The milkman _was_ just here and _forg_ot his cap.

It is Mom. Mom is _by_ the _door_ with the milkman's cap on top, a pan _of_ milk, and a black and white cat. Mom is like the milkman. Mom and the milkman _are_ alike when Mom has the milkman's cap on top.

The cat _wants_ its milk!

"Drink _your_ milk, Cat!" _said_ Mom.

The cat _wants_ more.

The cat _wants_ fish!

Mom _goes_ _to_ the inlet _of_ the lake with the milkman's cap still on top.

"Did _you_ _for_get _you_ had the milkman's cap on top, Mom?"

"Yes, _I_ _for_got the cap on top," _said_ Mom.

Mom fishes _for_ catfish and sunfish. The cat likes catfish, but Mom and Dad like sunfish. _Do_ the fish like hotdogs? Yes, the fish _do_ like hotdogs.

Mom got a fish that _was_ _kind_ _of_ black, with stripes, a "blackfish?" Mom _put_ the "blackfish" back in_to_ the lake.

Mom got a fish that _was_ _kind_ _of_ blue, with stripes, a "bluefish?" Mom _put_ the "bluefish" back in_to_ the lake.

Mom got a fish that _was_ _kind_ _of_ red, with stripes, a "redfish?" Mom _put_ the "redfish" back in_to_ the lake.

Mom got a fish that _was_ white, a whitefish.

"That is a fish!" _said_ Mom, but Mom still _put_ the whitefish back in_to_ the lake.

The "blackfish," "bluefish," "redfish," and whitefish _were_ still alive when Mom _put_ them back in_to_ the lake!

Mom gets _two_ fat sunfish. Yes!

Mom gets _one_ fat catfish. Yes!

"_Come_ along, Cat. Let us _put_ these fish on a hot fire," _said_ Mom.

But the milkman's cap went in<u>to</u> the inlet <u>of</u> the lake.

"<u>I</u> cannot get the cap with <u>my</u> hand," <u>said</u> Mom <u>to</u> the cat. "<u>I</u> cannot <u>do</u> a long-jump <u>to</u> get the cap."

Mom is sad.

The _two_ sunfish _are_ fat. The _one_ catfish is fat. Mom takes the fat fish _to_ the campfire. On the campfire, within the campfire, the fish get hot! The fish _are_ _done_.

"_Have_ a catfish, Cat!" _said_ Mom.

Mom and Dad _have_ sunfish. Mom, Dad, and the cat ate _their_ fish. The fish _were_ the best!

But, _where_ is the milkman's wet cap? Is it still in the inlet _of_ the lake?

<u>No</u>. Mom did fish the milkman's cap <u>from</u> the inlet <u>of</u> the lake with a stick, and the milkman came back <u>for</u> his cap.

Mom gave the milkman his wet cap. Mom is glad. The milkman is wet and glad.

Questions to check:

1. Who forgot his cap?
   a. the cat
   b. the milkman
   c. Mom
2. Who has the milkman's cap on top?
   a. the cat
   b. the milkman
   c. Mom
3. Who likes hotdogs? Who likes catfish? Who likes sunfish?
   a. the fish, the cat, Mom and Dad
   b. the cat, Mom and Dad, the fish
   c. Mom and Dad, the fish, the cat
4. Were the "blackfish," "bluefish," "redfish," and whitefish still alive when Mom put them back into the lake?
   a. no
   b. yes
5. Did the milkman get his cap back?
   a. yes
   b. no

STORY 2: DOLCH SIGHT WORDS

The _Eight_ Handmade Backpacks

COMPANION STORY 35: DOLCH SIGHT WORDS

Non-phonetic Dolch sight words:

are	_house_	_they_
back/_door_	_of_	_to_
_do_	_once_	_two_
does	_one_	_u/pon_
dog/_house_	_said_	_walk_
doll/_house_	_school_	_want_
	school/_house_	
door	_some_	_watch_
door/bell	_some/one_	_were_
eight	_some_/time	_where_
fire/_house_	_some/where_	_who_
have	thank-_you_	_you_
hen/_house_	the	_your_
hot/_house_	_their_	
	there	

Phonetic Dolch sight words (BUT phonics concepts not yet introduced):

a	_for_	_was_
all	_go_	_we_
both	_I_	_what_
_by_	_or_	

Phonetic words (but not Dolch):

back/pack	kids	sad
back/packs	last	self
glad	lot	sell
hat	lots	side
him/self	more	time
in/side	nine	times
kept	pack	trip
kid	packs	trips

Miscellaneous:

$$$ #1   #2   #4   #5   #9   #10

Dolch vocabulary to practice:

1. Before reading these words, write a list of the silent e words or have your mom or dad write the list while you read just the silent e words below. HINT: There will be an e at the end of the word,

but watch out, there might be an s or an 's added to the word after the e. WARNING: Some silent e words are hidden in a compound word.

2. Then read the words from the list in the back of the book while your mom or dad checks if you put each word on your list.   Did you find them all?

and	gave	it	tell
at	get	like	ten
back	got	made	thank
bell	grass	make	that
best	had	man	these
big	hand	man-made	this
blue	hand/made	not	those
bring	hands	on	top
bus	has	pig	went
but	hen	red	white
came	hill	ride	will
can	hill/top	ring	with
cap	him	stick	with/in
did	his	sticks	yes
dog	hot	store	
doll	in	sun	
fire	is	take	

Once *upon* a time, *some*time, *somewhere*, *there* *was* *someone* with *eight* handmade backpacks.

The handmade backpacks *were* the best! Those packs *for* *your* back *were* made *by* hand. *They* *were* handmade. *They* *were* man-made.

"Did <u>you</u> make those backpacks?" <u>said</u> a man with a big, red, white, and blue hat.

"Yes," <u>said</u> the backpack man, "<u>I</u> made these backpacks <u>by</u> hand."

"_Where_ _do_ _you_ _want_ _to_ _go_ with those backpacks? _What_ _do_ _you_ _want_ _to_ _do_ with those backpacks? _Where_ _do_ _you_ _want_ _to_ take those backpacks?" _said_ the man with the big, red, white, and blue hat.

"_I_ _want_ _to_ sell these backpacks at a store," _said_ the backpack man. "_Where_ is _there_ a store?"

"_I_ can tell _you_ _where_ _there_ is a store," _said_ the man with the big, red, white, and blue hat.

"This store is not within a _house_. This store is not within a fire_house_, a hot_house_, a dog_house_, a doll_house_, _or_ a hen_house_, but this store is _by_ a schoolhouse," _said_ the man with a big, red, white, and blue hat.

"This store is not on a hilltop, and this store _does_ not _have_ grass _by_ it, but this store has a _door_ with a _door_bell and a _door_ at the back, a back_door_," _said_ the man with a big, red, white, and blue hat.

The man with the big, red, white, and blue hat did _walk_ and the backpack man did ride _to_ the store that _was_ _by_ the _schoolhouse_. _They_ did _go_ _there_ _eight_ times, _eight_ trips, _to_ bring the _eight_ backpacks.

There _was_ a bus _by_ the side _of_ the _schoolhouse_. The bus had a bell on top. The store _was_ within the red, white, and blue bus. The _door_ _of_ the bus _was_ red. The bell on top _was_ red.

The man with the big, red, white, and blue hat went inside the bus. The backpack man went inside the bus with his _eight_ handmade backpacks.

Ten kids came _to_ the _door_ _of_ the bus with $$$ in _their_ hands.

"_Where_ _are_ the handmade backpacks?" _said_ the kids.

The backpack man gave _one_ backpack _to_ the big kid, _one_ backpack _to_ the kid with a cap, _one_ backpack _to_ the kid with a pig, _one_ backpack _to_ the kid with _two_ sticks, _one_ backpack _to_ the kid in the sun, _one_ backpack _to_ the kid with a ring, _one_ backpack _to_ the kid with a _watch_, and _one_ backpack _to_ the kid _who_ _said_, "Thank-_you_."

Two kids did not get backpacks. _They_ _were_ sad. The backpack man will _have_ _to_ make more backpacks _for_ those _two_ kids.

The backpack man made _two_ more
backpacks. The _two_ kids came
back _to_ the red, white, and blue
bus. The _two_ kids got _their_
backpacks. _They_ _were_ glad.
Their _two_ backpacks _were_ the
best _of_ _all_.

The backpack man kept the $$$ _for_ himself and _for_ the man with the big, red, white, and blue hat. The backpack man made lots _of_ $$$. The man with the big, red, white, and blue hat made _some_ $$$. _They_ _were_ _both_ glad.

Questions to check:

1. Who made the backpacks?
   a. the man with a big, red, white, and blue hat
   b. the kid with a pig
   c. the backpack man
2. Where did the backpack man want to go with his backpacks?
   a. a house
   b. a store
   c. a hill
3. The man with the big, red, white, and blue hat and the backpack man did go to the store _____ times.
   a. eight
   b. nine
   c. two
4. The backpack man made _____ backpacks in all in "THE EIGHT HANDMADE BACKPACKS."
   a. eight
   b. nine
   c. ten
5. Who did like their backpacks the best?
   a. kid #1 and #2
   b. kid #4 and #5
   c. the last two kids #9 and #10

STORY 3: PHONICS

The Caveman

COMPANION STORY 36: PHONICS

Non-phonetic Dolch sight words:

<u>do</u>	<u>of</u>	<u>there</u>
<u>does</u>	<u>once</u>	<u>they</u>
<u>door</u>	on/<u>to</u>	<u>to</u>
<u>door</u>/stop	<u>said</u>	<u>u/pon</u>
<u>goes</u>	<u>some</u>	<u>want</u>
<u>have</u>	<u>some</u>/thing	<u>where</u>
<u>live</u> (short i)	<u>some</u>/where	<u>who</u>
<u>lives</u> (short i)	the	

Non-Phonetic Words (phonics concepts not yet introduced):

a	<u>for</u>	<u>my</u>
a/rise	<u>from</u>	<u>no</u>
a/wake	<u>go</u>	<u>was</u>
a/woke	<u>he</u>	<u>what</u>
<u>be</u>	<u>I</u>	
<u>by</u>		

Phonetic vocabulary to practice:

1. Before reading these words, write a list of the silent e words or have your mom or dad write the list while you read just the silent e words below. HINT: There will be an e at the end of the word, but watch out, there might be an s or an 's added to the word after the e. WARNING: Some silent e words are hidden in a compound word.
2. Then read the words from the list in the back of the book while your mom or dad checks if you put each word on your list.   Did you find them all?

am	bed	cave/man
an	bed/time	cave/man's
and	best	chase
at	big	chick
ate	bone	chicks
back	branch	club
back/hand	but	Club
back/stop	cake	cup
bath	can	cup/cake
bathe	can/not	desk
bathes	cave	did
bath/tub	Cave	dog

elk	home/made	mill/stone
fast	hot	more
fish	hot/dog	munch
get	if	must
glad	in	name
gulch	in/side	not
gun	is	on
gun/shot	it	pan
hand	jump	pan/cake
hand/made	king	pig
has	king/fish	pink
help	lamp	pond
hen	land	quick
hid	like	ran
hide	likes	run
hides	lot	runs
hill	lots	sad
him	lunch	self
him/self	mad	set
his	made	shack
home	make	shine
home/land	man	shot
home/like	mill	shot/gun

side	sun/shine	tub
sink	sun/up	up
sit	swing	up/set
skunk	swings	use
skunks	take	wake
snack	takes	wakes
squid	taste	when
stink	then	will
stone	thing	wind (short i)
stop	things	wind/mill
strong	think	wish
strong/man	thinks	wish/bone
Strong/man	this	with
sun	time	yes

The man with a club _who_ _lives_ in a cave, the caveman, has a name. The man is strong. His name is Strongman.

"_I_ am strong. _My_ name is Strongman," _said_ Strongman.

Strongman _lives_ _by_ himself in a cave with his club. The name _of_ the caveman's cave is Cave. The cave _does_ not _have_ a _door_. The cave _does_ not _have_ a _door_stop. _There_ is _no_ _door_ _to_ stop!

The cave is _by_ a windmill with a big millstone. When the wind _goes_ _by_ the mill, then the stone inside the mill _does_ _go_ fast.

This is the caveman's homeland. Strongman likes his homeland. His cave is homelike. _There_ is a lamp and a desk. _There_ is _some_thing _to_ sit on. _There_ is a sink. _There_ is a tub. _There_ is a bed.

Sink and Tub

It is time _for_ a bath in the caveman's tub. The caveman takes his bath in his bathtub. The caveman bathes in his bathtub.

Then it is time _for_ bed. It is bedtime. The caveman _goes_ _to_ bed.

The sun is up. It is sunup. The sun will shine. _There_ will _be_ lots _of_ sunshine. The caveman wakes up with the sun. The caveman is awake. The caveman awoke at sunup. The caveman did arise.

Strongman likes _to_ swing his club with a backhand swing. The name _of_ his club is Club. Club is like a backstop. _No_ thing can stop Club! Chicks cannot stop Club! Skunks cannot stop Club!

Once *upon* a time, Strongman did *want* lunch and *to* use Club with a backhand swing at *some* chicks and *some* skunks. Strongman hid in back *of* the shack. The pink pig did make the chicks and skunks run *to* the pond.

Strongman _was_ sad. Strongman did not get lunch then. The fast pink pig _was_ quick. Yes!

Strongman did get _to_ use Club with a backhand swing at the skunk in the gulch. The skunk ran fast _to_ the hill. The skunk did jump _upon_ a branch. The skunk did not stink.

Strongman _was_ glad the skunk did not stink, but Strongman _was_ sad. _He_, _once_ more, did not get lunch!

The caveman is in his cave. _There_ is a hen and a skunk _by_ his cave.

Strongman did swing his club with a backhand swing at the skunk. Strongman did chase the skunk up on*to* a branch, but <u>once</u> more, Strongman did not get lunch.

Somewhere Strongman thinks _he_ can get lunch. Strongman swings Club with a strong backhand swing at a kingfish. Strongman ate the kingfish _for_ lunch with a homemade cupcake. _There_ _was_ a wishbone in the kingfish. Strongman did wish _for_ a hotdog.

Strongman swings Club at a squid.
Strongman will munch on squid,
not a hotdog, _for_ a snack with a
handmade pancake.

Strongman swings Club at an elk.
The elk is big. The elk runs at
Strongman.
"Help," _said_ the caveman.
Strongman runs _to_ his cave and
hides.

Strongman is mad. Strongman is upset. _Some_thing can stop Club! An elk can stop Club!

Strongman _said_, "_I_ must get a shotgun with gunshot in it if _I_ _want_ elk _for_ lunch. _I_ must _have_ a shotgun with gunshot in it if _I_ _want_ elk _for_ lunch."

Strongman _said_, "_No_, _I_ _do_ not _want_ a gun. _No_, _I_ _do_ not _want_ a shotgun with gunshot in it."

"_I_ _do_ not _want_ elk _for_ lunch if _I_ _have_ _to_ _have_ a shotgun with gunshot in it," _said_ Strongman.

Strongman is glad _for_ his kingfish and his squid! The caveman is glad _for_ his homemade cupcake and his handmade pancake _from_ the millstone in the windmill. _They_ taste the best.

Questions to check:

1. What is the caveman's name?
   a. Cave
   b. Club
   c. Strongman
2. Does the caveman's cave have a door?
   a. no
   b. yes
3. The caveman ate _____ and _____ for lunch.
   a. a skunk, chicks
   b. a kingfish, a squid
   c. an elk, a hen
4. What does the caveman wish for?
   a. a wishbone
   b. a hotdog
   c. a club
5. What two things did the caveman make from the millstone in the windmill?
   a. a homemade cupcake and a handmade pancake
   b. a club and a bathtub
   c. a sink and a bed

STORY 4: PHONICS

<u>Someone</u> <u>Who</u> Likes <u>to</u> Jump

COMPANION STORY 37: PHONICS

Non-phonetic Dolch sight words:

<u>are</u>	<u>one</u>	the
<u>do</u>	<u>out/put</u>	<u>to</u>
<u>floor</u>	<u>put</u>	<u>u/pon</u>
<u>house</u>	<u>said</u>	<u>watch</u>
in/<u>put</u>	<u>some</u>	<u>where</u>
<u>of</u>	<u>some/one</u>	<u>who</u>
<u>once</u>	thank-<u>you</u>	<u>you</u>

Non-Phonetic Words (phonics concepts not yet introduced):

a	<u>for</u>	<u>out</u>
a/cross	<u>I</u>	<u>was</u>
a/long	<u>my</u>	<u>what</u>
a/while	<u>my</u>/self	
<u>be</u>	<u>no</u>	

Phonetic vocabulary to practice:
1. Before reading these words, write a list of the silent e words or have your mom or dad write the list while you read just the silent e words below. HINT: There will be an e at the end of the word, but watch out, there might be an s or an 's added to the word after the e. WARNING: Some silent e words are hidden in a compound word.
2. Then read the words from the list in the back of the book while your mom or dad checks if you put each word on your list. Did you find them all?

and	dad	hand/stands
at	Dad	help
back	did	hit
back/pack	fun	home
bench	get	hope
bump	got	if
bumps	grass	in
cake	hand	in/side
came	hand/shake	it
can	hand/shakes	jump
can/not	hand/spring	land
cave	hand/springs	last
cave/man	hand/stand	like

likes	pack	springs
long	pan	stand
lot	pan/cake	stands
lots	path	thank
lump	sad	then
lumps	sat	this
mad	self	time
man	set	up
milk	shake	up/set
milk/man	shakes	well
mom	side	when
Mom	smile	will
more	smiles	yes
not	spot	
on	spring	

Handsprings _are_ fun. Handstands _are_ fun. Yes! Yes! Yes! Smiles and handshakes _are_ fun.

"_I_ like _to_ jump. _I_ like _to_ _do_ handsprings. _I_ like _to_ _do_ handstands. _I_ like smiles. _I_ like handshakes."

"_I_ can _do_ handsprings and handstands on the grass. _I_ can jump along the path. _I_ can jump across the path. _I_ can _do_ handsprings and handstands on a bench. _I_ can jump along the bench. _I_ cannot jump across the bench. _Once_ in awhile, _I_ can _do_ handsprings and handstands inside the _house_ on the _floor_."

"*Once* *upon* a time, *I* did not jump well. *I* did not *do* handsprings. *I* did not *do* handstands."
No *one* *said*, "Yes! Yes! Yes!"
"*I* did not get *one* handshake."

"*For* a long time, *I* *was* sad, and *I* *was* upset. *I* sat at home and did not jump. *I* sat at home and did not *do* handsprings. *I* sat at home and did not *do* handstands."

"_I_ got mad at _my_self. Then _I_ got more upset. _I_ can _do_ this. _I_ can jump. _I_ can _do_ handsprings. _I_ can _do_ handstands. If _I_ in_put_ lots _of_ time, the _output_ will _be_ smiles and handshakes, _I_ hope!"

Mom came _to_ help. Dad came _to_ help. "_I_ did lots and lots _of_ handsprings and handstands on the grass. When _I_ did land on the grass, _I_ did not get bumps. When _I_ hit the grass, _I_ did not get lumps."

"_Once_ in awhile, _I_ did lots _of_ handsprings and handstands inside on the _floor_."
Mom and Dad came _to_ help.
"At last, _I_ did lots more handsprings and handstands on a bench. _I_ did it! _I_ did it! _I_ did it!"

Handsprings _are_ fun. Handstands _are_ fun. Yes! Yes! Yes! Smiles and handshakes _are_ fun.
"_I_ like _to_ jump. _I_ like _to_ _do_ handsprings. _I_ like _to_ _do_ handstands. _I_ like smiles. _I_ like handshakes. _I_ in_put_ lots _of_ time, and the _output_ _was_ smiles and handshakes!"

"Thank-_you_, Mom and Dad!"

Questions to check:

1. If you do handsprings and handstands, what do you get?
   a. smiles
   b. handshakes
   c. a and b

2. Where can you do handsprings and handstands?
   a. on the grass
   b. on the floor inside the house
   c. along the path
   d. on a bench
   e. a, b, c, and d

3. If you do not do handsprings and handstands well, what will you not get?
   a. a watch
   b. smiles and handshakes
   c. a pancake

4. Who did help?
   a. the caveman
   b. the backpack man
   c. the milkman
   d. Mom and Dad

5. Where was the last spot to do handsprings and handstands?
   a. on the bench
   b. on the grass
   c. on the path
   d. on the floor inside the house

Glossary

Dolch/Sight Words: Words your child should first sound out, using phonics, and then master by sight, so sounding out is no longer necessary.

Phonics: A practice of sounding out words.

Consonants: Sounds, phonemes, which are blocked by the teeth, tongue, and/or lips. Sometimes it is just easier to think of consonants as all the letters that are not vowels: b, c, d, f, g, h, j, k, l, m, n, p, q, r, s, t, v, w, x, y (y can be a vowel or a consonant), and z.

Blends: Two or three consonants next to each other each of which make a sound, such as fl, pr, spr, st, str, and tr. The letter x is considered a blend because it makes the sound /ks/. The letters qu make the sound /kw/ and are also considered a blend.

Digraphs: Two consonants next to each other that make only one sound. The letters ch, sh, th, wh, and ng are digraphs.

Vowels: Sounds, phonemes, which are NOT blocked when pronounced. The vowels are a, e, i, o, u, and sometimes y.

Short Vowels: /ă/ as in apple, /ĕ/ as in elephant or Ed, /ĭ/ as in igloo or itch, /ŏ/ as in octopus, and /ŭ/ as in umbrella or up.

CK Rule: The sound of /k/ can be spelled with c, k, or ck. After a short vowel, the /k/ sound is spelled with a ck.

Floss Rule: The /f/ sound can be spelled with f or ff; the /l/ sound can be spelled with l or ll; the /s/ sound can be spelled with s or ss, and the /z/ sound can be spelled with and s, z or zz. After a short vowel /f/ is spelled ff, /s/ is spelled ss, /l/ is spelled ll, and /z/ is spelled zz. Those two letters (ff, ll, ss, zz) still only make one sound.

Use of s: s is added to nouns and verbs for syntax.

Use of 's: 's is used to indicate possession.

Use of es: To form a plural of a noun, usually add s. However, when a noun ends with s, x, z, ch, or sh, form the plural by adding es.

Silent e Rule: When an e is at the end of a word, it often causes the previous vowel to become long. For example, at becomes ate, mad becomes made, rid becomes ride, and us becomes use. Words such as Mae, lie, doe, and blue can also be considered to be following the Silent e Rule even though there is no consonant between the vowel and the final "silent" e.

Compound Words: A compound word is two or more words, each of which could stand alone, but, also, could be joined together, forming a new word often with a new meaning. Examples of compound words are landslide, milkman, and pancake. Words such as across, alike, and along are also classified as compound words because the <u>a</u> (short u (/ŭ/ as in umbrella /ŭ/ or up /ŭ/) as in "Once upon <u>a</u> time" can stand alone as a single word, but it can also be joined with cross (across), like (alike), and long (along) to form a compound word. A compound word can be written as a single word (handmade) or as a hyphenated word (first-class).

ABOUT THE AUTHOR/ILLUSTRATOR

Mary Schuler MA, specialized trainer/tutor, is an experienced and result-oriented special education teacher with over 50 years of experience in the special education field. Obtaining her B.A. in elementary education from the College of St. Catherine's in St. Paul, Minnesota, and her M.A. in Special Education, Schuler taught kindergarten, 1st grade, 5th grade, and special education in public school settings. While teaching and tutoring, she discovered that solving learning problems isn't accomplished by just requiring the students to do more schoolwork. She developed/founded the literacy, math, and writing foundational approach resulting in hundreds of students achieving academic and life success. She now works with parent reading coach to train/coach parents/teachers on the literacy, math, and writing foundational approach.

Nicholas Torres MEd, has over 20 years of experience in executive management. He built and led one of the largest and most nationally recognized human services organizations, founded and governed two charter schools, founded a nonprofit focused on scaling high impact social enterprises including school-based health centers and high school/college access and completion pipelines, and founded a social sector consulting organization. Currently, he is president of social innovations partners which publishes the social innovations journal and facilitates the social innovations institute & lab. He serves as adjunct faculty at University of Pennsylvania. He started parent reading coach with his colleagues because he believes parents and caregivers are the primary vehicles toward quality education and should have the educational tools and knowledge to educate their children.

Silent e List from Vocabulary Words

The Milkman's Cap
ate, blue, bluefish, came, fire, gave, here, like, likes,
live (long i), take, takes, these, white, whitefish

The Eight Handmade Backpacks
blue, came, fire, gave, handmade, like, made, make, man-made,
ride, store, take, these, those, white

The Caveman
ate, bathe, bathes, bedtime, bone, cake, cave, Cave, caveman,
caveman's, chase, cupcake, handmade, hide, hides, home,
homeland, homelike, homemade, inside, like, likes, made,
make, millstone, more, name, pancake, shine, side, stone,
sunshine, take, takes, taste, time, use, wake, wakes, wishbone

Someone Who Likes to Jump
cake, came, cave, caveman, handshake, handshakes, home,
hope, inside, like, likes, more, pancake, shake, shakes, side,
smile, smiles, time

Answer Key

The Milkman's Cap
1. **b) the milkman**
2. **c) Mom**
3. **a) the fish, the cat, Mom and Dad**
4. **b) yes**
5. **a) yes**

The Eight Handmade Backpacks
1. **c) the backpack man**
2. **b) a store**
3. The man with the big, red, white, and blue hat and the backpack man did go to the store **a) eight** times.
4. The backpack man made **c) ten** backpacks in all in "THE EIGHT HANDMADE BACKPACKS."
5. **c) the last two kids #9 and #10**

The Caveman
1. **c) Strongman**
2. **a) no**
3. The caveman ate **b) a kingfish** and **b) a squid** for lunch.
4. **b) a hotdog**
5. **a) a homemade cupcake and a handmade pancake**

Someone Who Likes to Jump
1. c) a and b
2. e) a, b, c, and d
3. b) smiles and handshakes
4. d) Mom and Dad
5. a) on the bench

Made in the USA
Middletown, DE
19 October 2022

12765569R00046